© 2019-2023 Chelsea Kong

All rights reserved. All images used in this book are licensed copies from their respectful owners including Freepik, Pixabay, Pexels, and myself. This book or any portion thereof may not be reproduced or used in any manner whatsoever without the express written permission of the publisher except for the use of brief quotations in a book review.

Printed in 2019-2023, made in Toronto, Canada
ISBN: 978-1-990399-65-7

God's favor is giving us more than what we ask.

It is all the best things that God wants to give us.

It is also what He wants to do for us.

Love God then He will give us His favor.

WHAT IS FAVOR?

It is to like somebody a lot and you want to do things for them.

It is more than what you would do for somebody else.

Favor can last for the rest of our life.

JESUS

Samuel had favor with the LORD and with men (1 Samuel 2:26)

Jesus also has favor with God and with people.

RECEIVE FAVOR

Favor comes from God and gives you what you want and need.

You can ask God to give you favor with people, at work, home, and anywhere.

"For he who finds me finds life
And obtains favor from the LORD"
(Proverbs 8:35)

He who finds a wife finds a good thing And obtains favor from the LORD. (Proverbs 18:22)

Esther won favor with the king more than the other woman (Esther 2:17).

POWER OF FAVOR

God's favor will make the horn of the people exalted (Psalm 89:17)

His favor blesses us with more than we need.

It gives us joy, peace, long life, and prosperity.

It protects us from our enemies and makes us free.

WHO CAN HAVE FAVOR?

God gives favor to those who have a blameless walk. (Psalm 84:11)

He will bless the people who do what is right in His eyes.

INCREASE AND PROMOTION

God was with Joseph and he had favor in all that he did.

He did all things that Potiphar made him in charge of everything in his home.

Washington was a President of the USA before.

Joseph also found favor with Pharoah.

He got an increase and was promoted.

RESTORATION

Favor gives you back what the enemy stole from you.

Israel had favor with the Egyptians that they gave them silver and gold.

HONOUR

Favor will give you honour.

Your enemies will see that you have honour.

Israel had honour before the Egyptians.

God can bring you to
a place of celebration.

INCREASE IN WEALTH AND LAND

God's favor is giving us more than what we ask. It is all the best things that God wants to give us. It is also what He wants to do for us. Love God then He will give us His favor.

Mordecai got everything that belonged to Haman.

GREAT VICTORY

His favor gives us a great victory even when the battles are hard to win.

God will make a way for us to win the battle.

He gave Israel victory over many battles against their enemies even when it looks impossible.

BEING CHOSEN

King Saul liked David
and let him serve him.

God knew David's heart and knew him.

IT MAKES YOU STAND OUT

God's favor makes us important among others.

Esther became important.

the king gave Esther special attention by treating her better than the other women.

REQUESTS GIVEN

God will give us what we ask Him to do.

We also will be given what we ask somebody else to do when God favors us.

Esther's request was done by the king.

CHANGE OF LAWS, RULES, AND MORE

Favor will change laws, rules, and more.

God can make His plan happen in replace of other plans.

VICTORY

God will fight the battle for us.

God will give us the victory even without having to fight.

WISDOM

Be like the
Proverbs 31
woman to be wise.

Fear God and
receive wisdom.

Fear God and receive wisdom.

Read Proverbs to know wisdom and become wise.

Ask God for wisdom.

READING

then God will work for you.

God will give us favor
when we focus on Him.

OPENS THE DOOR

Favor gives us miracles by
opening the way for us.

It goes with us wherever we go.

Other people can see God's favor on us.

We will have open doors
that other people do not have.

God's favor lasts forever.

Stay with the Lord and enjoy it.

SALVATION PRAYER

God, I know I sinned against you. Forgive me for the wrong that I have done. I believe that Jesus Christ died on the cross for me. That He rose from the grave so that after three days. I can have His long-lasting life. Come into my heart to be my Lord and Savior. I choose to turn away from my sins and I choose to follow you. Lead me to walk with you. Keep me safe and teach me your ways. Stop every bad thing in my life that has an open door to hurt me. Close those doors. Holy Spirit fill me now in Jesus' name. Amen.

BAPTISM IN THE HOLY SPIRIT 🔥

Jesus, you are the one that fills me with Your Spirit. Come Holy Spirit and come into my life and fill me to overflow with Your presence. Come with your fire too. Thank you for the gift of tongues in Jesus' name. Amen.

Open your mouth and let the words come out that God gives you. It will be words that you don't know what they mean. You can ask God what it means. You need to let Him talk through you every day to grow this gift.

He will bring you closer to God and you will know Jesus more. You will have power from God to do great things and know things.

PRAYER

Father God, I want to know how to walk in your favor. Thank you for your favor. Open the doors that nobody can open. Close the wrong doors. Make a way that I will meet the right people and to have every blessing and thing you have for me. Give me wisdom to walk in your ways and live a life full of your favor. Thank you for the increase. Thank you for the right people in my life in Jesus' name. Amen.

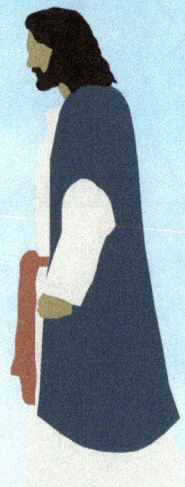

Message from the Author

God's favor gives us unlimited blessings. It has no limits. When we obey God, He will give us favor. Then we will have all the blessings and whatever we want. He will give us everything we need and more than that. He will also protect us and people will know that God is with you. You will always get the best and be the head and not the tail. Learn to walk in favor. His favor brings the supernatural into our life.

We can also have double favor like it says in 2 Corinthians 1:15. We must expect the supernatural to happen. We must be ready for favor to be given and keep our promise. Treat others the way you want to be treated. Stay in the fear of the Lord and obey Him. Then He will reward you.

OTHER PRODUCTS

- Knowing God
- How to Hear God's Voice
- New Life in Jesus
- Loving Israel
- God's Gifts
- Meeting God
- Word Power
- Fruit of the Spirit
- The Tabernacle
- Bride for Jesus
- A Life of Prayer
- Live Free
- Who am I in Jesus
- Walk in Love
- God's Favor
- Man of God
- Woman of God
- How to Use Money
- God's Wisdom
- Fasting
- See Jerusalem and Bethany
- First Fruit Offering
- Feast of Trumpets
- Day of Atonement
- Feast of Tabernacles
- Counting the Omer
- Festival of Lights
- Glory, Presence, and Holy Spirit
- Live in God's Presence
- 31 Day Devotional
- Biblical Puzzle Book Vol 1
- Biblical Puzzle Book Vol 2
- Biblical Puzzle Book Vol 3
- Biblical Puzzle Book Vol 4
- Biblical Puzzle Book Vol 5
- Bible Puzzles for Young Children Book 1
- Bible Puzzles for Young Children Book 2
- Bible Puzzles for Young Children Book 3
- Biblical Puzzle for Children Books 1-3
- How God Speaks
- Knowing Jesus
- Knowing Holy Spirit

OTHER PRODUCTS

Teaching Series
How to Hear God's Voice Teaching Guide & Audio Book
Relationship with God, Jesus, Holy Spirit Guide
Knowing God, Jesus, Holy Spirit Guide & Audio Book

Teaching (Non-Sale)
Purim
Passover
Resurrection

More books to come!

MORE BOOKS ON AMAZON, KOBO, AND BARNES AND NOBLE
HTTPS://CHELSEAK532002550.WORDPRESS.COM/

Review

More books on Amazon, Kobo, and Barnes and Noble
https://www.amazon.com/author/chelseakong

Please leave a review and share with friends to help the author continue to write more books to reach more readers. Thank you so much for your support.

OTHER BENEFITS

If you would like to contact the author, you can email:
kayunkk@gmail.com

You can also check out my YouTube channel found on my website. Please remember to subscribe and share with others.

You will also find free books on my website. Each teaching series has additional information explained in the audio books.

Review

Remember to review on Amazon, Barnes and Noble, and share on social media with your family and friends to help spread the news. Your reviews will help many others who need to read these books.

About
CHELSEA KONG

She is a writer, creative arts and digital media artist, skilled administration professional, and podcaster. Chelsea also served in a variety of roles, from audiovisual, photography, to assisting on the worship team, and ministry team. She also has a passion for families being united.

Chelsea has been a guest on Unity Live Radio and The Lady Tracey Show and is highly recommended by a Proud Christian blog. She graduated from Hotel and Restaurant Management, Digital Media Arts, Office Administration, and experience working with children. Chelsea lives in Toronto, Canada. She mainly writes children's books, stories, bridal writing, poems, lyrics for songs, words of encouragement, blessings, prayers, and jokes. The author of How to Hear the Voice of God, the Bridal Collection, Knowing God, etc. She also has her own Bible Puzzle books and other inspired products. Her podcast channel is called Chelsea K on Anchor, Spotify, and iTunes.

Please check my website to find out more:
https://chelseak532002550.wordpress.com/

www.ingramcontent.com/pod-product-compliance
Lightning Source LLC
Chambersburg PA
CBHW060414010526
44107CB00006B/692